A Children's History of Portugal

By Sérgio Luís de Carvalho
Illustrated by António Salvador

Translated by Inês Lima

Table of Contents

We are going to tell you the history of Portugal!

Countries, just like each one of us, have their own history. They were born, they developed over the years, and they had good times and bad times. However, unlike the history of a person, the history of a country is very long, spanning many years and even centuries.

Now, the story that we are about to tell you is the story of a very old country, one of the oldest in Europe. This country is almost one thousand years old. But for many years before this country was founded, many people passed through the land and lived in this place. The knowledge that these people left behind can still be seen today.

In this way, Portugal is the result of the work and of the experience of many people. And it is for this reason that we can say that Portugal is a rich country: rich in history, in monuments and in many other things that those who came before us, our ancestors, left to us. They left us this country of Portugal and, one day, we will leave it to those who will come after us.

Let us tell you the long history of Portugal. As you read these pages, you will hear us talk about many people and the things that they did, and you will learn about what the Portuguese accomplished over the course of all those years. Sometimes, you may not understand a word or two, but do not worry. At the end of each chapter of the book, you will find a list of difficult words, along with an explanation of their meanings. We will also tell you some interesting stories in these lists. If you still have questions about a word or a phrase, you can ask your teachers, your parents or even an older brother or sister for an explanation. They would certainly be happy to help you.

Now that we have told you these things, we hope that you will have fun reading this book and that you may learn something new from it in the process.

Happy reading!

Sérgio Luís C.

The First Inhabitants: the Lusitanians

The Lusitanians were one of the first peoples, over 2,000 years ago, to inhabit the territory that now makes up a large part of Portugal. We don't know much about the Lusitanian people and most of the little that we do know comes from ancient Roman historians. According to the Romans, the Lusitanian people were skilled at war. Their warriors used a small, round shield to protect themselves from the arrows and spears that were thrown at them by their enemies. They protected their bodies with a thick cloth of linen, and they wore a metal or leather helmet on their heads. They also wore leather on their legs for protection. They wielded daggers, swords and spears made of iron.

Roman historians also describe some of the curious habits of the Lusitanian people. For example, they would first take steam baths by throwing cold water onto rocks that had been heated by fire. They would then take a cold bath.

We also know that the Lusitanians ate only one meal per day and that their food was very simple. They usually drank water, and they rarely drank beer or wine. They made their bread from acorn flour, and they also used butter and salt. They sat in a circle when they ate and passed the food around from one to the other. But the elders were served first.

The Lusitanians lived in round, stone houses with a thatched roof made from culm straw. Men wore dark clothes and women wore colorful clothes. They slept on straw on the floor and used only a mantle to cover themselves. Both men and women had long hair. When men went to war, they tied their hair with a band.

The Lusitanians exercised, competed in races and danced in circles to the sound of flutes and horns with men and women holding hands. When someone became ill, the sick person was left by the side of a road so that they could speak to people passing by and ask for advice from anyone who had suffered from a similar illness.

Tribes would unite when they were attacked

The Lusitanians lived in tribes[1] and these tribes were often rivals with each other. However, when they were attacked, they would unite. One of the main activities of the Lusitanians was the herding of cattle. Because the Lusitanians lived in most of the territory that Portugal occupies today, some historians believe they are the ancestors of the Portuguese people.

---

1 Tribe: A group of people living in a village under the command of a chief.

Lusitanians
in their village

The Romans

About 2,000 years ago, the armies of the Roman Empire invaded the Iberian Peninsula.[1] This empire was one of the most powerful in the world and it ruled over most of Europe. However, it was not easy for the Romans to conquer the lands of the Lusitanians. The Lusitanians fought the Romans and they often won. One Lusitanian chief became very famous for his resistance to the Romans—his name was Viriatus. Nevertheless, as time passed, the strength of the Roman army eventually won out.

After they conquered the Iberian Peninsula, the Romans brought great progress to these lands. They built roads, bridges and aqueducts[2] and they developed commerce, crafts[3] and agriculture. They founded cities where life was busy with theaters, hippodromes,[4] baths[5] and temples. The ruins of some of these cities can still be seen today, such as Miróbiga (close to Santiago do Cacém) and Conímbriga (close to Coimbra). You can also see other kinds of Roman ruins that are relatively well preserved, such as Diana's Temple in Évora, the Roman Theater in Lisbon, the Vila Formosa bridge at Ponte de Sor, the baths at São Pedro do Sul, the bridge at Chaves, the ruins at Pisões in Beja and the Roman objects in the Odrinhas Museum at Sintra.

One of the most important legacies of the Romans was their language, Latin

The Romans divided the Iberian Peninsula into three provinces.[6] One of these provinces was called Lusitania, which corresponds, for the most part, to the territory occupied today by Portugal. The Romans also left us their laws, which were very advanced for that time.

Nevertheless, one of the most important legacies of the Romans was their language. In fact, the Portuguese language that is spoken today developed from the language spoken by the Romans, which was Latin. The Latin language changed over the centuries and gave rise to other languages, such as Spanish, French, Italian and Romanian.

As the centuries passed, the relationship between the Romans and the ancient peoples of the Iberian Peninsula became more peaceful. The ancient peoples began to follow Roman customs and began to use their language and follow their laws. They started to live in the cities the Romans had built, and they traveled on Roman roads and bridges.

In the meantime, during the fourth century (about 1,700 years ago) the Romans became Christians. Because of this, we can say that the Romans brought Christianity to Portugal and most Portuguese people continue to follow this religion today.

---

1 Iberian Peninsula: The territory occupied by Portugal and Spain.
2 Aqueduct: A built structure that conveys water over great distances.
3 Crafts: A term applied to activities done by hand, without the help of machines. This includes pottery, basketry and carpentry, among others.
4 Hippodrome: The space where horse races took place.
5 Baths: Places where people treated themselves with the curative and hygienic powers of water.
6 Province: Territories administered by a governor, who represents the central authority of a king or emperor.

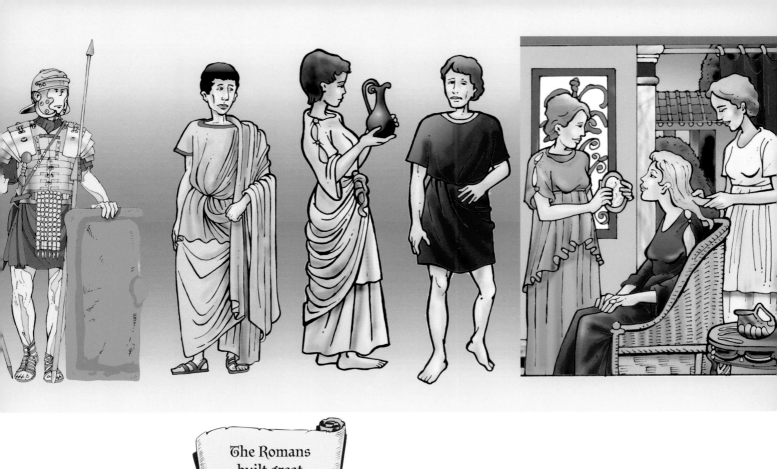

The Romans built great works

The Visigoths

The Roman Empire stretched across most of Europe, as far as modern Germany, and occupied North Africa and the Middle East. However, as time passed, this great empire began to have more and more problems. There were several different peoples who tried to invade it from beyond the empire's borders. The Romans called these peoples barbarians.[1]

As time went on, these so-called barbarian peoples continued to put more and more pressure on the empire's borders. During the fifth century (about 1,600 years ago), several peoples entered the Roman Empire and settled in the old Roman provinces. In this way, the Roman Empire eventually disappeared. What happened at this time to the Iberian Peninsula and to the province of Lusitania?

The main "barbarian" people to settle in the Iberian Peninsula were the Visigoths. In the sixth century, the entire peninsula was ruled by the Visigoth monarchy.[2] For the first time, the Iberian Peninsula was a single kingdom under the authority of one king. In order to govern the territory, the king received help from several noblemen,[3] who were given important territories to administer.[4] At times, the power of these noblemen became so great that it weakened the authority of the king. Because of this, there was some instability[5] and even some revolts[6] during the rule of the Visigoths.

The Visigoths adopted a few Roman customs. They admired Roman construction and Roman forms of organization, and they began to imitate the lifestyle of the Romans. One of the Roman legacies that the Visigoths adopted was the Christian religion, which meant that the Church began to play a larger role in society. The Church helped the Visigoth kings with government and it played an important role in education and culture. The Church also tended to the needs of the poor and the sick.

The weakening and fall of the Visigoth monarchy

However, with the passing of time, the Visigoth monarchy began to grow weaker. The nobles, who should have helped the king, began to rebel with more frequency, trying in this way to gain more power. These rebellions weakened the power of the Visigoth kings.

In the year 711 (around 1,300 years ago), other people, Muslims from North Africa, invaded the Iberian Peninsula. They took advantage of the divisions and the rebellions among the Visigoths. Their arrival and the length of time they remained here were very important to the history of Portugal.

---

1 Barbarian: Today, the word "barbarian" means someone who is rude and aggressive. But the Romans used it to refer to people who did not speak Latin or Greek.
2 Monarchy: The type of government in which the king occupies the highest position. In general, when a king dies, his eldest son inherits the position.
3 Nobles/Noblemen: People born into a family holding a title of nobility, such as count, baron or duke. In the past, these families had many privileges and held the most important positions in the kingdom.
4 Administer: To manage a territory, that is, to make decisions so that everything functions well.
5 Instability: A situation of great anxiety. There is instability in a country when there is disorder, discontent or serious problems.
6 Revolt: To rise in rebellion; to reject the authority of a government and try to put an end to it.

The Visigoths arrive on the Íberian Peninsula about 1,400 years ago

The Muslims

Muslims believe in the religion known as Islam.[1]

In the year 711, a Muslim army invaded the Iberian Peninsula by crossing the Strait of Gibraltar.[2] This army defeated the Visigoths and occupied almost the entire Iberian Peninsula. We say almost all of it because, in reality, a small portion of the territory in the north of the peninsula resisted the invaders. In this territory, Asturias, located in northern Spain, Christian Visigoth knights continued to fight. A few years later, they slowly started to reconquer land that had been lost to the Muslims.

From the eighth century onwards (about 1,300 years ago), the Iberian Peninsula was almost completely under Muslim rule. The Muslims were a cultivated and advanced people. Their presence in Portugal was positive. They developed agriculture by introducing the watermill,[3] the noria[4] and the dam,[5] and they cultivated fruits, such as lemons, oranges,[6] mulberries and apricots. They also developed crafts and pursued a number of scientific disciplines (medicine, geography, astronomy[7] and mathematics), which were useful for the future navigations made by Portuguese sailors. They were talented artists and they left an interesting heritage that includes a number of buildings they constructed in several cities and villages.

The Muslim heritage contributed to the development of Portugal

The Portuguese language contains several words that derive from Arabic, the language spoken by the Muslims. Some examples are: zero, alicate (pliers), argola (ring), andaime (scaffolding), algarismo (digit), armazém (warehouse), arsenal (armory), arroz (rice), xarope (syrup), azeite (olive oil), açucar (sugar), laranja (orange), tremoço (lupine bean), lima (lime), tambor (drum), almirante (admiral), and azeitona (olive). In total, the Portuguese language has about one thousand words of Arabic origin. The names of many villages and cities in Portugal are also Arabic. These names often begin with "al." In this way, the Muslim heritage contributed to Portugal's future development and the Portuguese language.

Do you remember when we said that several Visigoth warriors had taken refuge in Asturias in northern Spain? Well, sometime after the Muslim conquest, these Christian Visigoth warriors began to reconquer some of the territory lost to the Muslims, moving from the north to the south. It was a difficult and slow process. It took several centuries until the Christians were once again able to take control of the entire Iberian Peninsula. Over the course of centuries of fighting, Christians and Muslims experienced times of war and times of peace. However, as time went by, the process of reconquering land by the Christians became nearly unstoppable. It was in the midst of these wars between Christians and Muslims that the future kingdom of Portugal was born.

---

1 Islam: Religion that originated in the Arabian Peninsula in the seventh century (about 1400 years ago) with Muhammad as prophet. Islam is among the religions with the most followers in the world, including in Portugal.
2 Strait of Gibraltar: A narrow strait (or channel of water) separating North Africa and the Iberian Peninsula.
3 Watermill: A mill whose wheel is moved by flowing water.
4 Noria: A device for raising water from a stream or river with a series of pots or buckets that revolve around a wheel driven by flowing water.
5 Dam: A barrier constructed of stone or wood to hold water back and raise its level.
6 Orange: Here is a fun fact! In the Arabic language, Portugal means "land of oranges".
7 Astronomy: The science that studies the planets, such as their location in the sky and their movements. Astronomy should not be confused with astrology, which studies signs of the zodiac.

The Muslims left an important heritage

The Condado Portucalense

As we have told you, the Visigoth warriors started to reconquer territory that had been lost to the Muslims in 711. Slowly, they began moving from the north to the south. Because of this, the Iberian Peninsula became divided into two parts, with Christians in the north and Muslims in the south. But Muslims still lived in areas controlled by Christians and Christians lived in areas controlled by Muslims. In general, both communities tolerated[1] each other.

This process of reconquering land had advances and setbacks, and there were even periods when the two peoples lived together in relative peace. Nevertheless, the Christians continued slowly to advance down the territory. As they were moving south, they created independent Christian kingdoms. One of these was the kingdom of León, located in northern Spain.

But a problem arose as these changes were taking place. How could a king govern territory that had just been reconquered? Indeed, roads, means of transportation and of communication[2] did not exist then as they do today. Roads were difficult and dangerous, and travel was very slow. This was one reason that kings, such as the king of León, needed the help of noblemen to assist him in ruling different parts of his kingdom. The king would give a piece of land to a nobleman who, in exchange, was expected to govern it according to the king's wishes. When a nobleman died, responsibility for governing the land was usually passed on to his eldest son.

Dom[3] Henrique was appointed by the king of León to govern the Condado Portucalense

Within the kingdom of León, located between the rivers Douro and Minho, was a region called the Condado[4] Portucalense. This territory was ruled by a count, who followed the king's orders. In 1096 (over 900 years ago), the king of León appointed D. Henrique to administer the Condado Portucalense. He was obliged not only to defend this territory from Muslim attacks, but also to advance south to conquer new land.

However, D. Henrique had larger ambitions. He wished to increase the autonomy[5] of his territory and even to make it independent. However, the count, D. Henrique, died in 1112. Thus, the task of gaining independence for the Condado Portucalense fell to his young son, D. Afonso Henriques. This young infante[6] is important in this history because he later became the first king of Portugal.

---

1 Tolerate: When two people or communities accept each other without great competition or hostility.
2 Means of communication: Different ways to establish contact over distances. This could include phones, fax machines, mail and email.
3 Dom: Title used to address nobles and members of the Portuguese royal family. It is usually abbreviated as "D."
4 Condado: County. A territory governed by a Count.
5 Autonomy: A region has autonomy, or is autonomous, when it can govern itself. It is close to being independent.
6 Infante: An old word used for royal children.

GUIMARÃES

BRAGA

ORTO

COIMBRA

Count D. Henrique
governed the Condado
Portucalense

D. Afonso Henriques, the First King

D. Afonso Henriques was still young when his father died and he was called to govern the Condado Portucalense. The infante had inherited from his father the same desire to make the Condado Portucalense an independent kingdom. However, this was a very difficult task. First, the young count had to obey the king of León, who held ultimate authority over the Condado Portucalense. In addition, he had to fight the Muslims, who threatened his territory. Nevertheless, D. Afonso Henriques did not give up.

The first thing that he did was to gather all of the noblemen around him in the Condado Portucalense, organize an army, and fight those who, within the Condado Portucalense itself, were opposed to his authority. In 1128, he won one of his first battles, the Battle of Saint Mamede, and, in this way, he became the leader of the Condado Portucalense.

The first king of a new kingdom: Portugal

After this happened, D. Afonso Henriques began to challenge the authority of the king of León, while he also continued to fight the Muslims in the south. After a few years and many battles, he finally achieved his goal. In 1143 (over 850 years ago), the king of León was forced by the Treaty[1] of Zamora to recognize D. Afonso Henriques as king of a new kingdom called Portugal.

However, there was still much to be done.

In the south, the Muslims controlled much territory and they occupied several villages and cities. Now, as king of Portugal, D. Afonso Henriques could focus all of his energy on the conquest of those lands. Year after year and battle after battle, the kingdom of Portugal continued to grow.

The cities of Santarém and Lisbon were conquered in 1147, Beja in 1162, and Évora in 1165. In 1179, toward the end of his reign, King D. Afonso Henriques received a letter from the pope which recognized Portugal's independence. The pope was a very important person and had much more power at that time than he has today. For this reason, it was very important that the pope recognized Portugal as an independent kingdom. The pope who did this was named Alexander III.

D. Afonso Henriques had obtained Portugal's independence by fighting the king of León, conquering nearly the entire area of central and southern Portugal, and obtaining the pope's recognition.

Because of these things, we can say that Portugal was born with King D. Afonso Henriques.

---

1 Treaty: A written agreement between two rulers or two countries.

What the First Kings of Portugal Did

After the death of King D. Afonso Henriques, the tasks that Portugal's first kings had to perform were difficult. They had to govern the new kingdom and, in order to do this, they asked for help from representatives of the nobles, the clergy,[1] and the people. After listening to their advice and their complaints in meetings, called the *cortes*, or "courts," the kings would make their decisions. However, since the Portuguese population in those days was small and spread out, Portugal's kings also made an effort to settle, or populate,[2] the territory, something which contributed to the defense and development of the kingdom.

Another important task was maintaining Portugal's independence because Muslims continued to fight in the south. They made frequent attacks and even succeeded in retaking villages and cities in the Algarve and Alentejo regions. For this reason, Portugal's southern border was unstable. However, the Portuguese slowly won back territory and villages. They never gave up fighting.

Finally, in 1249 (over 750 years ago), King D. Afonso III conquered the last villages that were still under the control of the Muslims: Faro, Albufeira and Silves. It was also during D. Afonso III's reign that Lisbon[3] was made the capital of Portugal.

The Spanish are defeated at the Battle of Aljubarrota

However, Muslims were not the only ones who threatened the new country's independence. The kings of Spain still wished to reign over Portugal once again. Many wars were fought between Portugal and Spain because of this. One of the most important wars took place between 1383 and 1385. At that time, the king of Spain invaded Portugal with a large army. Portugal was in great danger, especially because the Portuguese army was much smaller. However, the Portuguese people supported their king, D. João I, and they won great victories. One of the greatest victories over the Spanish was the Battle of Aljubarrota. This victory strengthened Portugal's independence and banished the threat from Spain for many years to come.

Portugal's first kings were D. Afonso Henriques, D. Sancho I, D. Afonso II, D. Sancho II, D. Afonso III, D. Dinis, D. Afonso IV, D. Pedro I, D. Fernando I and D. João I. After D. João I's victories, Portugal's independence became more secure, and a new era dawned for the country.

---

1 Clergy: Members of the church.
2 Populate: When people move to and settle in places where there are few people living there.
3 Lisbon: Before Lisbon became the capital of Portugal, the king and his companions travelled across the country, staying for a few months in the main cities.

The first kings tried to develop the new kingdom

What Was Life Like During the Time of Portugal's First Kings?

During the time of the first kings of Portugal, life was very different from what it is today. Modern conveniences did not exist. For example, there were no machines and no electricity. Roads were bad and there were no easy means of communication. Most people died without ever having left the town where they were born, for trips were time consuming and complicated. The workday began at sunrise and ended at sunset. Medical care was very basic and nutrition was poor. Because of this, people died from diseases that are easy to treat today. Half of the population died before reaching adolescence,[1] and those who made it to adolescence rarely lived past the age of 40 or 50.

Most people worked in agriculture

Most of the population could not read or write, and those who wished to study had to do so in churches or convents.[2] This is one way in which the Church played a very important role at the time. Since most educated people belonged to the Church, it was often members of the clergy who helped the kings and who wrote the most important books. Books were written by hand in convents, which made them rare and expensive. The Church was also responsible for assisting the poor and the sick. The first university, called the General Study (Estudo Geral), was founded in Lisbon by King D. Dinis in 1290 (over 700 years ago). Later on, this university would move to the city of Coimbra.

Most people worked in agriculture and they lived off of the land. Because of this, many more people lived in the countryside than in the cities. When someone needed something, such as clothes, tools, guns or furniture, they had to go to artisans[3] to buy it. Stores like the ones we have today did not exist. Few people dedicated themselves to non-agricultural activities, such as fishing, crafts and commerce.[4] Commerce took place mostly in markets and fairs in cities and villages. But goods could also be purchased from sellers who travelled throughout the lands of the country.

The basic meal consisted of bread and wine. Most people ate little more than this, but at times meals could also include meat (pork, rabbit, chicken or beef), eggs, milk, and some fruit but few vegetables. Because of this basic diet most people were not in good health, and, if the land was not productive during one year, people would go hungry. Many things that we eat today were unknown to the Portuguese living at this time, such as turkey, potatoes, beans, corn, tomatoes, chocolate and tropical fruits.[5] Spices (pepper, curry, cloves, nutmeg, and more) and sugar were also quite rare and expensive.

This kind of life, which was very different from the way we live today, went on for many centuries with few changes.

---

1 Adolescence: The stage of life after childhood and before adulthood.
2 Convents: Buildings where members of the church live as a community, working and praying together.
3 Artisan: A person who practices a trade or craft.
4 Commerce: The exchange or buying and selling of goods.
5 Tropical fruits: Fruits from warm climates, such as kiwi, pineapple, mango, custard apple, papaya and banana.

Almost all products were bought at markets in towns

What Was the World Like at That Time?

We are approaching the time when the Portuguese set out to navigate the seas in an attempt to find other lands. But before we tell you about the voyages of the Portuguese, we wonder, what did people know about the world 600 or 700 years ago? They knew very little. Because of this, they had some strange ideas about the world around them. If you don't believe it, then pay attention…

People mostly lived on their lands and they rarely traveled. Those who did travel and who knew more about other lands, still knew little beyond the countries that were close to their own. Europeans were familiar with other parts of Europe and with North Africa, and they knew about the existence of parts of Asia. But the rest of the world was a mystery to them.[1] They knew very little about the seas and the oceans. Ships were fragile, sailing instruments[2] were poor, maps were rare and the maps that did exist were not very accurate.

This lack of knowledge gave rise to fear. Some said that the oceans were dangerous and they imagined that terrible monsters lived in them. Others believed that the seas were constantly boiling or that the seas were covered in so much darkness that ships would get lost on them. But there was also much curiosity about the seas and the oceans. What existed beyond the coasts of Portugal? Who lived in those lands? What treasures could be discovered there? How could ships sail to those distant shores?

The Portuguese were knowledgeable about nautical science

As you can see, curiosity was one of the factors that inspired the Portuguese to venture out into the world, but there were other reasons as well. The desire to obtain wealth in other lands and to spread the Christian religion throughout the world were important factors that we should remember. Another factor that enabled the Portuguese to explore the seas before other people did was the fact that they were knowledgeable about nautical science.[3] The Portuguese had received a number of important sailing instruments, such as the compass, from the Muslims. In addition, Portugal's location along the sea made it easier for them to begin their navigations.

Nevertheless, it is important for you to know that sailing voyages at this time were dangerous. Shipwrecks happened frequently, and sailors died on ships because of bad hygiene[4] and poor nutrition.[5] There were also pirates. Because of all this, you can imagine how much courage was needed to sail the seas in those days. Yet, despite all these dangers, Portuguese ships set out on the adventure of the seas, the adventure known as the Discoveries.

---

1 The American continent, Oceania and most of the African continent were unknown at the time to Europeans. They were, of course, known to the people who lived in those places.
2 Sailing instruments: Implements or devices used to guide people at sea, such as the compass or the astrolabe.
3 Nautical science: Knowledge and techniques related to sailing.
4 Hygeine: Conditions or practices that promote good health.
5 Poor nutrition: Most sailors ate only bisuits (a type of bread that was cooked twice), dried meat or dried fish, and water. Water went bad easily and became undrinkable. Refrigerators did not exist at this time.

People frequently feared the unknown sea

The First Voyages and the First Conquests in the Atlantic and along the Coast of Africa

The first phase of Portuguese overseas expansion consisted of seizing North African cities that were under Muslim rule. In 1415 (about 600 years ago), Ceuta was taken. However, the Portuguese had much larger ambitions. The next phase of expansion involved the discovery of new lands in the Atlantic Ocean and exploration of the coast of Africa.

The actions of the Infante D. Henrique, King D. João I's son, were very important during this early phase of overseas expansion. He gave direction to this movement. Under his guidance, the archipelago[1] of Madeira (in 1419) and the archipelago of the Azores (in 1427) were discovered and explored. The African coast was explored in the following years with ships advancing farther south every year. The Portuguese learned more about the African continent as they continued to travel down the coast. They passed Cape Bojador (in today's Western Sahara) in 1434 and Cape Branco (close to Mauritania) in 1441 and they reached the Cabo Verde islands in 1444, Siera Leone in 1460 and São Tomé and Príncipe in 1471.

The Portuguese built fortresses along the African Coast

Sailing had many dangers. Ships were fragile and storms were threatening. Even so, year after year Portuguese ships sailed into waters along the coast of Africa that were unknown to Europeans. These ships brought pepper, cotton, fish oils, whale oils, ivory, parrots, gold and slaves back to Portugal. In order to facilitate commerce with the people they encountered, the Portuguese built fortresses along the coast of Africa. These fortresses were known as factories, or trading posts, where the Portuguese exchanged the goods they brought with them from Portugal for goods that the local peoples brought to them. The most important fortresses were located on the coast of West Africa in Arguim (in Mauritania) and São Jorge da Mina (in Ghana).

While the coast of West Africa was being explored, the Portuguese continued to conquer cities in North Africa. A number of cities in this region were conquered by King D. Duarte, the son of King D. João I, and especially by King D. Afonso V, the son of King D. Duarte. However, these cities were difficult to take and, on a number of occasions, the Portuguese were defeated by Muslim armies and they failed to obtain the riches that they were seeking. But interest in voyages of exploration continued to grow.

The kings that were responsible for the early phases of Portuguese overseas expansion were D. João I, D. Duarte and D. Afonso V.

---

1 Archipelago: The name for a group of islands.

The Portuguese conquered Ceuta in 1415

Discovery of the Maritime Route to India

We have already mentioned that spices were highly appreciated in Portugal. However, they were very expensive because they came by land from India to Europe. Because the trip from India was long and dangerous, the price of spices was quite high by the time the spices were sold in Europe.

This is why King D. João II (the son of D. Afonso V) thought of a plan. Toward the end of the fifteenth century, over five hundred years ago, D. João II considered the possibility of reaching India by sea and of bringing spices to Europe on Portuguese ships. In this way, Portugal could make a huge profit. But how could India be reached by sea? No one knew the way. Even so, King D. João II was not discouraged. He believed that Portuguese ships could sail south along the coast of Africa until they reached the end of the African continent where they would then round the cape, head north, enter the Indian Ocean and reach India.

King D. João II ordered ships to explore the coast of Africa to see whether his plan could be followed. One of the sailors who led these expeditions was Diogo Cão. Another was Bartolomeu Dias, who passed the southernmost point of Africa (The Cape of Good Hope) and showed that it was possible to sail around Africa and reach India by sea.

The Treaty of Tordesillas was signed in 1494

During this time, Spain also wanted to expand its territory and reach India by sea. However, the king of Spain was not aware that the Portuguese already knew the way. In order to avoid conflicts, the kings of Spain and Portugal agreed to a treaty: they divided the world between them into two large areas. All the discoveries made in one area would belong to Portugal, while the discoveries made in the other area would belong to Spain.

This was the famous Treaty of Tordesillas, which was signed in 1494. Acting with prudence[1] and cleverness, King D. João II successfully had India placed in the area given to Portugal.

Shortly after this treaty was signed, King D. João II died. His successor[2] now had the task of sending Portuguese ships to India. King D. Manuel I prepared a fleet of ships to sail to India. It was led by Admiral[3] Vasco da Gama. His fleet arrived in India in May 1498. The riches of India and of Asia could now reach Europe through Portugal.

Between the end of the fifteenth century and the first half of the sixteenth century, under the leadership of Kings D. João II and D. Manuel I, Portugal reached the high point of its power and expansion.

---

1 Prudence: Acting with skill, caution and good judgement.
2 Successor: The person who occupies a position after another person leaves it.
3 Admiral: The highest rank in the navy.

The Portuguese in Asia

After Vasco da Gama arrived in India, the Portuguese were able to settle in Asia. The famous spices then began to arrive in Portugal. This brought great wealth to the country. However, the Portuguese were not satisfied doing business only with India. They also started to explore the southeastern coast of Africa, where Mozambique is now located. They sailed to the Persian Gulf, the Red Sea, and the Arabian Sea. During the sixteenth century the Portuguese continued to sail throughout Asia, reaching China, Myanmar, Indonesia, East Timor and even Japan.

In fact, the Portuguese were the first Europeans to reach Japan. And, you might be interested to know that the Portuguese introduced firearms to the Japanese archipelago. Another fun fact is that the Japanese language has many words of Portuguese origin, while the Portuguese language contains many words of Japanese origin.[1]

A great variety of goods were brought back to Portugal

By sailing throughout the Indian Ocean, from Mozambique to Oceania, the Portuguese were able to bring a great variety of goods to Portugal. In addition to spices, their ships transported silks, silver, gold, coffee, varnishes, perfumes, horses, pearls, cotton, cereals, sugar, precious stones, porcelains and rare woods.

As you can see, Portugal established an empire in the Indian Ocean, which historians call the Portuguese Empire in Asia. This empire was run by a governor, known as a viceroy,[2] who lived in India. He was responsible for overseeing trade, for providing protection for those engaged in the spreading of Christianity and for guaranteeing defense from enemy attacks.

One of the most famous viceroys was Afonso de Albuquerque. In the beginning of the sixteenth century, he organized the areas under Portuguese control, made great conquests and won important battles. Portuguese ships were constantly being attacked by enemies who also wanted to control trade and wealth in Asia.

Even though the Portuguese had fewer men and ships, they succeeded in defeating their adversaries[3] throughout the first half of the sixteenth century (the 1500s).

---

1 A few Portuguese words of Japanese origin are: biombo (folding screen), banzé (loud noise and confusion), catana (sword), chá (tea), chávena (small cup), cana (cane).
2 Viceroy: A person appointed by a king to govern a country or province belonging to his kingdom.
3 Adversary: Another word for an enemy or an opponent.

The Portuguese
were also in Asia

Brazil

On their long and dangerous voyages around the world, the Portuguese went beyond Africa and Asia. Although Portugal's population was small, a great number of ships sailed from the docks of Lisbon.

One of the lands the Portuguese sailed to was Brazil. Pedro Álvares Cabral was the navigator who first made the journey to Brazil in the year 1500. The first contact with the indigenous[1] population was friendly.

This first encounter was characterized by curiosity since the indigenous Brazilians knew nothing about the existence of the Portuguese and the Portuguese knew nothing about the Brazilians. They exchanged presents and then some Portuguese sailors spent a few days in an indigenous village, while some Brazilians spent some time on board the Portuguese ships.[2] That was the beginning of a great friendship that has lasted until the present day.

Friendly relations with Brazil endure to the present day

A few years after they arrived, the Portuguese realized that this new land, which they called Brazil,[3] offered many riches. Therefore, the kings of Portugal started to organize the territory to bring these riches, such as wood, cotton and sugar, to Portugal. They later discovered gold, but we will tell you more about that later.

In Brazil, the land was worked by slaves who had been brought over from Africa, mainly from Angola. Because of the presence of these slaves, there is a very important African influence in Brazil. This can be seen, for example, in Brazilian music and dance.[4]

It is important that you know that the Portuguese sailed around the world and, as they did this, they placed many different peoples under Portuguese authority for several centuries. These peoples eventually achieved independence from Portugal, but it is because of this long experience that Portuguese is the official language of eight countries: Portugal, Brazil, Angola, Mozambique, Guinea-Bissau, Cabo Verde, São Tomé and Príncipe, and East Timor. Today, Portuguese is one of the most spoken languages in the world.

Did you know that the country with the greatest number of Portuguese-speaking people is Brazil?

We would like to remind you that the kings governing Portugal at this stage of imperial expansion were D. João II and D. Manuel I. With them, Portugal reached the highest point of its power.

---

1 Indigenous: People originally from a certain area. It is similar to the word native.
2 An interesting episode from this time of first contact was when a Brazilian first saw a chicken. He was at first scared by it because chickens were unknown in Brazil and the indigenous Brazilians had never seen one before.
3 Brazil: The noun Brazil referred to a heavy, red wood that the Portuguese brought back from this land. Since this wood was as red as burning coal (brasa, in Portuguese), they named the territory Brazil.
4 Dance: African influence can be seen in several music styles and dances, such as capoeira and samba.

In 1500, Cabral's fleet reached Brazil

Portugal Lags Behind

The period of Discoveries and the riches that came to Portugal caused changes to the country. Science in Portugal made important advances. Astronomy, natural sciences, geography, cartography[1] and mathematics developed as Portuguese navigators sailed around the world. They discovered things that were unknown until then, such as new lands, new peoples and new forms of orientation at sea. The Portuguese showed that the earth is round, that the entire Atlantic Ocean is sailable, that people could live in the hottest places on earth, that India could be reached by sea and that a continent (America) separates Europe and Asia. In other words, the Portuguese helped to make many advances in science. Because of this, new ideas and new ways of thinking emerged. However, there were also signs that Portugal was falling behind other European countries. Even though much wealth entered the country, Portugal did not know how to take advantage of it. Portugal produced little and people purchased most of what they needed from other countries. People's lives, especially those of the poor, improved very little. There was some luxury, especially at the royal court,[2] but the Portuguese were squandering their fortunes. At the same time, other countries began to pursue overseas expansion. In the beginning, there was the Spanish, but then the Dutch, the French and the English became involved. As the sixteenth century progressed, Portugal lost its control over trade in the Indian Ocean and of the wealth of Asia.

Some people were afraid of new ideas

Portugal also began to have its own problems. Some people were afraid of new ideas and this brought about a time of repression.[3] In 1536, a religious court named the Inquisition, also known as the Holy Office, was established in Portugal. Because the Inquisition feared that new ideas were disturbing the population and putting the Catholic religion in danger, it persecuted anyone who had progressive ideas or religious doubts or who believed in other religions (Jews, Muslims and Protestants). Many books and thinkers were censored.[4] Many people were arrested, others were sent into exile[5] and hundreds were executed. This atmosphere of repression and censorship was a big setback to Portugal's development.

By the end of the sixteenth century, Portugal was in difficult circumstances. The empire was going through hard times and it brought less wealth to Portugal. In an attempt to revitalize the empire, King D. Sebastião invaded North Africa, but he died fighting Muslims in the Battle of Alcácer Quibir (in Morocco). To make matters worse, the king had gone off to war without having an heir to the throne. His great uncle, Cardinal D. Henrique, succeeded D. Sebastião as king, but he died two years later without an heir. Who would be the next king of Portugal?

The kings who ruled Portugal during this period of decline were D. João III, D. Sebastião and D. Henrique.

---

1 Cartography: The science of making and studying maps.
2 Royal court: The king's household.
3 Repression: The use of violence against people who disagree with certain ideas or practice certain acts. It is done as a way to control people.
4 Censor/Censorship: To prevent the spreading of certain ideas by prohibiting the sale of books, deleting parts of texts before they are published or stopping people from writing.
5 Exile: Voluntary or forced absence from your country usually because you are being persecuted.

The Ínquisition opposed new ideas and persecuted other religions. Ín 1578, D. Sebastião died in the Battle of Alcácer Quibir

From the Time of the Spanish Occupation to the Restoration of Independence

As we have told you, Portugal was in a difficult situation by the end of the sixteenth century. King D. Sebastião's death in North Africa made the situation even more complicated. The king had died in 1578 without leaving an heir to the throne. His great uncle, Cardinal D. Henrique, succeeded him as king, but he was an old man and he died two years later, in 1580, without an heir.

Without any descendants to inherit the throne, who would be the next king of Portugal?

As you might know, when a king died, his eldest son usually inherited the throne. If the king had no children, then his closest relative (a brother, grandson, or uncle, etc.) would become king. Because of this, when D. Henrique died, the strongest candidate to take the Portuguese throne was the king of Spain, for he was the son of a Portuguese princess and a grandson of King Manuel I.

The king of Spain, soon to be known as King Philip I of Portugal, seized the opportunity. He invaded Portugal, defeated the weak resistance put up by some Portuguese, and became king. As a result, Portugal and Spain were united.

This union of Portugal and Spain lasted 60 years. During this time, Portugal had three Spanish kings: Philip I, Philip II and Philip III. However, things did not improve for Portugal. Spain's enemies became Portugal's enemies and they attacked Portuguese territories in Brazil, Africa and the Indian Ocean. Portugal was now forced to participate in Spain's wars. At the same time, the kings of Spain did not seem to be concerned with what was happening in Portugal. As you can imagine, dissatisfaction began to spread in Portugal.

It was time for Portugal to regain its independence

In 1640, a group of Portuguese decided that it was time for Portugal to regain its independence and to break its union with Spain. To achieve this, they rebelled, expelled the Spanish governor and occupied Lisbon. They then proclaimed[1] a new king of Portugal.

Who was this king? It was the Duke[2] of Bragança, a descendant of Portuguese kings, who now became King D. João IV. The country accepted the new king and Portugal's independence was restored.[3]

However, Spain did not accept this situation. War broke out between the two countries, and it lasted for 28 years, ending only in 1668, after a number of Portuguese victories.

The Portuguese kings who ruled during this critical period were D. João IV, D. Afonso VI and D. Pedro II.

---

1 Proclaim: To announce.
2 Duke: A title of high nobility. It is usually associated with the offering of a piece of land by the king to a nobleman. In this case, the land was Bragança.
3 Restore: To return something to the way it was before. In this case, to make Portugal an independent kingdom, as it used to be.

Portugal Tries to Develop

Portugal went through a difficult period during the seventeenth century. The war with Spain had just ended, agricultural production was declining, there was very little industry and the once great Portuguese empire, which had dominated Asia, was now weak. Portugal's survival depended on purchasing products abroad, especially from England, which had become a great world power.

It was at this time that several kings decided that changes must be made. They thought of implementing reforms[1] to improve the situation. The first measure they took was to try to create industries in Portugal so that the country could produce more goods and not have to buy them abroad. They opened factories to produce wool and silk textiles,[2] and others to make hats and glass. Industries were established for naval construction and for steel production. In addition, new laws were enacted to prevent the Portuguese from buying foreign products. Improvements were also made to education, since there was a lack of educated people and skilled technicians. Other areas targeted for improvements were commerce, fishing and wine production.

A large part of Lisbon was rebuilt by Pombal

One of the outstanding figures of this period of reform was the Marquis[3] of Pombal, who served as prime minister[4] to King José I. Pombal was a determined[5] man, who did not hesitate to repress those who opposed his measures. Even today we can appreciate some of Pombal's actions. A large part of Lisbon, such as the downtown area known as Baixa, including Rua do Ouro, Rua da Prata, the Praça do Comércio and other nearby streets, was rebuilt according to Pombal's orders, after the earthquake of 1755 destroyed a significant part of Lisbon. He reacted quickly to this tragedy and had the city reconstructed with large avenues and houses built to resist earthquakes. As you can see, he played an important role in the development of the country.

It was also during the eighteenth century that the Portuguese started to exploit Brazil's riches, bringing gold, silver and precious stones[6] to Portugal. During this same period many missionaries[7] went to Brazil to spread the Catholic faith among the indigenous peoples. After India, Brazil became the most important territory of the Portuguese empire.

The Portuguese kings who ruled during this period were D. Pedro II, D. João V and D. José I.

---

1 Reform: A series of actions and measures taken in an attempt to improve something.
2 Textile: A cloth produced through weaving.
3 Marquis: A title of high nobility. As we have seen, these titles were associated with lands that were given by the king to a nobleman. In this case, the land was Pombal.
4 Prime Minister: The most important person appointed by the king to help govern the country.
5 Determined: A person who acts with certainty and confidence.
6 Precious stone: A precious stone is a very valuable stone, such as a diamond.
7 Missionaries: Priests who bring religion to distant lands in an attempt to convert the people there.

The Marquis
of Pombal tried to
develop Portugal

New Ideas and New Invasions

I n the eighteenth century, new ideas were spreading across Europe and they also made their way to Portugal. These ideas included demands for more freedom, for laws that were equal for everyone and that kings should no longer make decisions on their own, that the government should be shared with other people.

At this time, kings in Europe and in Portugal held all power in their hands. They made all of the decisions and only had to listen to a few advisors. For this reason, the old "courts" (*cortes*), where representatives of the church, the nobility and the people gave their opinions and voiced their complaints to the king, ceased to exist.

As you can imagine, the kings did not like these new ideas, which were being talked about and spread in cafes, academies,[1] newspapers[2] and, especially, among the most educated people and those with money (the so-called bourgeoisie[3]).

Many countries declare war on France

At the end of the eighteenth century, in 1789, a revolution[4] took place in France. This revolution, known as the French Revolution, removed the French king from government and implemented the new ideas that we just told you about. Throughout Europe, kings were afraid that the French Revolution might reach their own countries and, for this reason, they declared war on France. However, the French resisted these advances and soon began to invade other countries. One of these countries was Portugal. Why Portugal? Because it was an ally of France's greatest enemy: England.

When the French invaded and occupied Portugal in 1807, Queen D. Maria I and the heir, Prince D. João VI, had already fled to Brazil to avoid being put in prison. In response, England sent troops to Portugal and formed an army together with Portuguese soldiers. This army won many battles and defeated the French. In 1811, the French threat finally came to an end.

We might think that Portugal's problems had been solved, but they were not. Even though the French had been defeated, the English remained in Portugal. Meanwhile, D. João VI, who had become king of Portugal, was still in Brazil. As you can imagine, the situation was still very difficult for the Portuguese, because the English now controlled Portugal, commanded the army and made the best business deals for themselves. The Portuguese continued to be unhappy.

The rulers of Portugal during this period were Queen D. Maria I and King D. João VI.

---

1 Academies: Places where people met to discuss science and culture.
2 Newspapers: The first Portuguese newspaper was called the *Gazeta de Lisboa* and it appeared in 1715.
3 Bourgeoisie: Members of the middle class.
4 Revolution: A revolt. A situation when things change very quickly and, sometimes, in a violent way.

A Revolution and a Civil War: A New Portugal Is Born

As we saw, the situation in Portugal continued to be difficult. Many Portuguese were unhappy. The king remained in Brazil and the English were governing Portugal. Then, in 1820, a group of people defending the new ideas that we discussed in the previous chapter decided that they needed to start a revolution in Portugal.

And so they did. The revolutionaries triumphed and formed a new government to put their beliefs into practice. They wrote new laws that applied to everyone, approved the freedom of the press[1] and passed a new constitution.[2] They also asked King D. João VI to return to the country, which he did in 1821. But one year later, in 1822, Brazil became independent.

However, some people did not agree with the transformations that had taken place. Many noblemen and members of the church thought that the revolution had taken away their old rights and they started to organize themselves to fight the new government of 1820 and the new constitution. In fact, they wished to return to the time when the king held absolute power and they enjoyed more rights and privileges than the rest of the people.

The Portuguese were divided in their support of the king's sons

The situation became even more complicated in 1826. D. João VI died in this year and the Portuguese population took sides in support of one of his two sons. Those who supported the constitution and the new ideas it contained were called liberals, and they supported D. Pedro. Those who were against the new constitution and defended the old ideas were called absolutists, and they supported D. Miguel.

Taking advantage of the fact that D. Pedro was in Brazil, D. Miguel became king, revoked the constitution, brought back the old ideas and persecuted[3] the liberals. Many liberals were sent to prison; some were killed and others left the country and went into exile.

However, D. Miguel's victory lasted only a few years. The liberals formed an army under the command of D. Pedro and they arrived by boat on Portuguese shores in 1832. D. Miguel's army gathered itself to fight them. A civil war[4] began between the two armies and it lasted two years, ending in 1834. During this time, the country was divided between the liberals, those who supported D. Pedro and the new ideas, and the absolutists, those who supported D. Miguel and the old ideas. At last, after many battles, D. Miguel's army was defeated and he went into exile.

With the victory of the liberals, we can say that a new Portugal was born, a country with new ideas and the desire to develop along the same path and at the same rate as other European countries.

---

1 Press: Everything that is published in order to be read by the general public. This includes newspapers and magazines.
2 Constitution: The most important law of a country. The first Portuguese constitution dates from 1822.
3 Persecute: To harass or punish.
4 Civil war: A war within a country between people from this same country.

Portugal Focuses on Development, Once Again

After the civil war, a different kind of Portugal came into being. Kings no longer held all the power, and they now had to obey the most important law of the country: the constitution. Many things changed for the better, but many problems remained. Let's look at the things that changed.

As you may remember, Portugal's development was delayed in comparison with the rest of Europe. Agricultural production was poor and industry was underdeveloped. There were few means of communication. Poverty made many people leave Portugal to look for work in other countries. For all these reasons, in the second half of the nineteenth century, Portugal made a new effort to develop. What did the country do?

Since few means of communication existed, the railway became one of the areas that was developed the most. The first railway line was opened in 1856 between Lisbon and Carregado. A few years later, it was expanded to the north, to the south and to Spain. The railway grew with such speed that, forty years later, it stretched for more than 2,000 kilometers (about 1,243 miles) across the entire country. New roads and new bridges were also built. In addition, the postal service and the telegraph[1] and, later on, telephone services developed. Industry also grew. Many factories were built, especially factories making textiles, tobacco, ceramics, cork and glass.

The number of schools and students increases

At the same time, the educational system expanded. The number of schools and students increased and, because of this, illiteracy[2] slowly decreased. In fact, illiteracy has always been a serious problem in Portugal. The main cities had street lights, and newspapers and magazines brought news of the latest fashions coming from abroad, which wealthy people tried to imitate. Portugal also tried to develop its colonies[3] in Africa, particularly in Angola and Mozambique. After its experiences in India and Brazil, Portugal now focused on developing its African colonies with the purpose of extracting more wealth from them.

However, despite these efforts, Portugal was still less developed than other European countries and was unable to solve some of its problems.

The rulers during this period were Queen D. Maria II, D. Pedro V and D. Luís.

---

1 Telegraph: An old system of communication over great distances. It is not often used today.
2 Illiteracy: Illiteracy means not having the ability to read and write.
3 Colony: Territory that is not independent and is ruled by another coutnry.

Factories, bridges, trains... Portugal continued to develop

How the Monarchy Ended in Portugal

Do you remember when we said that Portugal had made many advances, but that some areas remained underdeveloped and a number of problems still existed? This was the situation the country was in at the end of the nineteenth century. Emigration[1] continued because poverty was very serious in many areas, especially in the countryside. Governments spent too much money and then found it difficult to manage the country.

On top of this, the government had borrowed money to make all of the improvements we spoke about in the last chapter. However, it was very difficult for Portugal to pay that money back.

Because of these circumstances, many people continued to be unhappy. How could the government resolve this situation? Unfortunately, it was not able to fix these problems. The governments continued to change, but the problems remained.

The Republic was established in Portugal in 1910

It was at this time that a political party emerged saying that these problems would be solved by ending the monarchy and replacing it with a Republic.[2] This party was the Portuguese Republican Party, which started to gain increasing amounts of support in the cities of Lisbon and Porto.

In 1890, another event occurred which brought even more discontent to the people and made them believe that the monarchy was incapable of finding a solution to Portugal's problems. What happened was that Portugal wanted to occupy the entire region between Angola and Mozambique, but England wanted to do the same thing. Because of this conflict, England sent a message to the Portuguese government saying that Portugal had to leave that territory and if it did not, then England would declare war on Portugal. The Portuguese government agreed and abandoned the region.

This decision outraged the Portuguese people. For many, this was proof that Portugal was losing power and they held the monarchy responsible for the decline. The king at this time was D. Carlos I and he became increasingly unpopular, while the Republican Party was gaining more support. A few years later, in 1908, D. Carlos I was assassinated in Lisbon, along with his eldest son and heir to the throne, D. Luís. The king's youngest son then became king as D. Manuel II. However, D. Manuel II ruled for only two years. On October 5, 1910, a revolution in Lisbon put an end to the monarchy. The king went into exile in England and the Republic was established in Portugal. The national anthem and national flag were chosen during this period.[3]

---

1 Emigration: When people leave their own country and move to another one. People often emigrate in search of work.
2 Republic: A form of government in which people vote for their national representative through elections. An elected President can only hold office for a few years.
3 The Portuguese national anthem is very patriotic. It celebrates Portugal and criticizes England.

In 1908, D. Carlos was assassinated and, in 1910, the Republic was proclaimed

The First Years of the Portuguese Republic

The first President of the Portuguese Republic was Manuel de Arriaga. The Republican governments wrote a new constitution and a number of laws to improve the living and working conditions[1] of the Portuguese people. They also developed the African colonies and improved education by increasing the number of schools and founding new universities. People had more freedom along with a new lifestyle and new fashions in clothing. Cinema[2] also developed at this time and sports, such as football (or soccer), gained popularity. The Republicans made great efforts to develop the country.

However, they also had to face many problems. One problem was that the laws the Republicans passed displeased many people. The Church, for example, believed these Republican laws went against religious teachings.[3] In addition, there was much political instability. Most Republican governments lasted a very short time. Supporters of the monarchy staged revolts in an attempt to restore the monarchy. Even the Republican party was divided between groups with different ideas. As dissatisfaction grew, more and more workers went out into the streets in protest and the number of strikes[4] increased.

The First World War started in 1914

To make matters worse, the First World War began in 1914. Countries such as England, France and Russia were on one side of the conflict, while Germany, Austria and Turkey were on the other side. In 1916, Portugal entered the war on the side of England and its allies against Germany. Why? Because Portugal was afraid of losing its African colonies, which were being attacked by Germany. Portugal sent soldiers to fight in Angola, Mozambique and Europe. When the war ended in 1918 with the defeat of Germany, Portugal was able to retain its African territories.

However, one of the consequences of the war was that many products became more expensive, while there were shortages of other products. Workers continued to protest, and instability continued. Many people began to wish for a government that would rule with more authority[5] and that would use violence, if necessary, to solve problems.

This is what happened in 1926. Part of the army rebelled and established a dictatorship[6] in Portugal. This new form of government was expected to solve the country's problems. But was it able to solve them all?

---

1 Working conditions: This is the situation in which people work, including working schedules, amount of pay, hygiene and safety and security in the workplace, and more.
2 Cinema: Movies at this time were in black and white and without sound.
3 The Church disagreed with several laws, such as the one allowing divorce. It also opposed the Republicans for persecuting members of the Church and for trying to make it more difficult for the Church to continue its activities.
4 Strike: When workers stop working as a form of protest against something.
5 Authority: Governing with authority means demanding obedience and doing what is necessary to get it.
6 Dictatorship: A form of government in which the ruler has complete authority. In a dictatorship people are not allowed to express their opinions freely, especially if they criticize the government.

Developments were being made in cinema, while Portuguese soldiers bravely fought in the First World War

Salazar's Dictatorship

In 1926, a dictatorship was established in Portugal. Many people were satisfied, because they believed a powerful government could solve Portugal's problems. The person in charge of the government was Professor Oliveira Salazar. Ruling as a dictator, Salazar was able to improve the country's situation, especially its economy.[1] Thanks to his actions, the country entered a more stable[2] and peaceful period.

Salazar tried to develop the country by building new roads, dams and public buildings, such as courts of law and schools. He also passed new laws and a new constitution. Unlike the previous Republican governments, Salazar always tried to obtain the Church's support.

The Second World War began in 1939. Portugal did not enter the war and, because of this, it was one of the few neutral[3] countries in Europe between 1939 and 1945 where there was peace.

There was no freedom in Portugal under Salazar's regime

However, there was a serious problem with Salazar's dictatorship: there was no freedom in Portugal. The press and the arts were censored[4] and political parties were banned. Those who disagreed with the government had to remain silent; otherwise, they could go to prison or lose their job. Many people had to leave Portugal and live in exile. Those who decided to resist the dictatorship were imprisoned, and some even died in jail, where they were sometimes mistreated. In addition, it was impossible to remove Salazar from government because there were no free elections. There were several revolts against the dictatorship, but these were put down by the government.

A persistent problem was the fact that Portugal continued to be less developed than other European countries. The population, especially those living in the countryside, faced many hardships and this caused emigration to increase. Education did not improve as much as it should have. The number of schools and the number of students increased, but illiteracy remained very high.

However, the biggest problem was yet to come. In 1961, many Angolans started a rebellion to demand their independence. Since Salazar refused to grant independence to any Portuguese colony, the Angolans decided to revolt and start a guerrilla war.[5] Shortly after that, rebellions and guerilla fighting broke out in Mozambique and in Guinea-Bissau. Salazar sent troops to fight the guerillas,[6] but the war did not come to an end. Many thousands of young Portuguese soldiers were sent to fight in Angola, Mozambique and Guinea-Bissau. The war continued for many years, but no one was able to claim victory.

---

1 Economy: Everything related to money, finances and the wealth of a country.
2 Stability: When the situation of a country is calm and quiet.
3 Neutral: When a country during a war does not support either side.
4 Censor/Censorship: The government made newspapers change articles or would not allow articles to be published. Certain songs could not be sung, certain books could not be published and often journalists and artists were sent to prison.
5 Guerrilla war: A type of war in which one side makes a surprise attack, but then flees in order to avoid direct confrontation against the enemy. This type of warfare is very exhausting for those being attacked and can result in many victims.
6 Guerrillas: Soldiers who fight in a guerrilla war.

The colonial wars and a lack of freedom were two big problems during the dictatorship

The End of the Dictatorship and the Beginning of Democracy

By 1968, Salazar was an old man and became seriously ill. He was then replaced as leader of the government by Professor Marcelo Caetano.

During his first few years in office, Marcelo Caetano gave the impression that the dictatorship was going to become more relaxed. Some even believed that this political regime would come to an end. In fact, most people hoped for these kinds of changes. However, as time passed, these wishes were not realized. People were being sent to prison for opposing the regime, censorship continued, and elections were still not free. Even though repression[1] was not as severe as it had been during Salazar's time, the truth was that Portugal continued to be ruled by a dictatorship.

Meanwhile, Professor Marcelo Caetano tried to expand the country's development so that it would not be as far behind other European countries. Industry grew and more attention was given to the poor.

However, Portugal's most serious problem was the colonial wars in Africa, where guerilla fighting continued in Angola, Mozambique and Guinea-Bissau. The government was spending large sums of money on the army, which meant that little money could be used to help further develop the country. At the same time, almost all other countries condemned Portugal for not granting independence to its colonies in Africa. In addition, it started to become clear that Portugal could not possibly win these wars.

In the last years of the dictatorship, especially after 1973, average Portuguese citizens were not the only ones tired of the war. Many members of the Portuguese military felt the same way. Some military officials began to meet secretly to plot against the regime. What did they wish to achieve? They wanted three things: to end the war and grant independence to the colonies; to transform Portugal into a democracy;[2] and to develop the country.

The military occupies the streets on April 25, 1974

Finally, on April 25, 1974 the dissatisfied elements of the military rebelled and occupied the streets of Lisbon, the main military bases,[3] and other important places, such as radio stations, airports and the country's borders. The government of Marcelo Caetano fell and the dictatorship came to an end.

The military established democracy in Portugal. The country was now ready to start a new era, the one in which we live today.

---

1 Repression: The control of political, social, or cultural freedoms by force.
2 Democracy: A form of government in which there is freedom and people freely elect their representatives. Today Portugal's government is a democracy.
3 Military base: A building where soldiers work and where military equipment and arms are located.

Democracy arrived in Portugal on April 25, 1974

Portugal in Recent Years

I t is now time to talk about contemporary Portugal and its democracy and freedoms. But you should remember that Portugal has only enjoyed these freedoms for a little more than 40 years, because these were established on April 25, 1974. After this date, Portugal became a democratic country and it granted independence to the African colonies. It has also continued to develop since then. Let's take a closer look at how this happened.

Democracy: April 25 brought freedom of speech,[1] the freedom of assembly[2] and freedom of the press.[3] Political freedom was established and political parties began to emerge. They can now participate in free elections to elect the President of the Republic as well as other elected officials throughout the country.

Decolonization: Democracy brought the war to an end and began the process of decolonization.[4] During 1974 and 1975, independence was granted to Guinea-Bissau, São Tomé and Príncipe, Cabo Verde, Angola and Mozambique. The process of decolonization did not always go well. Many Portuguese living in the colonies feared what might happen to them and they returned to Portugal, often under difficult circumstances. Another problem was that new wars began in some of these newly independent African countries. The most serious was in Angola, where the civil war lasted for many years. Another critical situation was that of East Timor, which was invaded by Indonesia. After many years of fighting, East Timor finally achieved its independence.

Portugal enters the European Union

In 1974, Portugal was one of the least developed countries in Europe. In 1986, Portugal decided to join the European Union. By doing this, Portugal was able to receive large sums of money to help with its development. This allowed Portugal to grow and to address many of its issues.

Many other things changed as well. More people had access to education and more students started to attend universities.

Most people now have access to new technologies (computers, TVs, mobile phones and smart phones). The Portuguese can afford to buy things that they previously could not, and the latest fashion trends reach Portugal quickly. The position of women has also begun to improve. Women enjoy more freedom now than they did before the arrival of democracy.

However, despite the progress that has been made, much remains to be done for Portugal to become as developed as the most advanced European countries.

Hard work and education will help Portugal continue to make great strides forward. Even you can play a role. Do you think you can?

---

1 Freedom of speech: The right to express opinions and have ideas.
2 Freedom of assembly: The right to meet with other people to discuss ideas and opinions. It includes the right to create political parties and associations.
3 Freedom of press: The right of newspapers, publishers, and TV and radio stations to report and express opinions and ideas.
4 Decolonization: When a country becomes independent from another country that used to govern it.